Instant Filipino Recipes

My Mother's Traditional Philippine Food
In a Multicooker Pot

ELIZABETH ANN BESA-QUIRINO

PHOTOGRAPHS BY CONSTANTE G. QUIRINO

FILIPINO COOKBOOK RECIPES
FROM ASIAN IN AMERICA

Produced and printed in the United States of America.

ISBN: 9781723844805

Copyright © 2018 Besa-Quirino LLC. All rights reserved.
Author: Elizabeth Ann Besa-Quirino
Associate Editor: Elpidio P. Quirino
Copy Editor: Paola Paska
Assistant Editor: Constante G. Quirino
Book Design: Triple Latte Design
Photography by Constante G. Quirino
Food-styling by Elizabeth Ann Besa-Quirino
Photographs of Lourdes "Lulu" Reyes Besa, Luz Jugo Reyes and Ponciano Reyes Sr. by Bob's Manila, Veluzar Photography Philippines and courtesy of the Gualberto Besa Family Library.
Author's Photo: Fordyce Studio, New Jersey, USA

Instant Pot is a registered trademark of Instant Pot Company which is not associated with this book.

Disclosure: The author was not paid to review or endorse the brand and product Instant Pot or any multi-cooker.

Praise & Accolades

This book is a timely and delightful gift from beloved author and respected food journalist Elizabeth Ann Besa-Quirino. As the respected culinary historian and blogger behind "Asian In America" and the author of two cookbooks, Betty Ann has welcomed countless readers and cooks into the Filipino kitchen, presenting classic dishes, illuminating ingredients, and demystifying techniques she learned as a child in her mother's Filipino kitchen. She's also shared her creative solutions to the everyday challenges of cooking for her family in her busy American home kitchen. In this book, *Instant Filipino Recipes: My Mother's Traditional Philippine Food in a Multicooker Pot*, Betty Ann takes the next step, sharing how today's popular multicooker helps her bridge the gap between the traditional time-consuming cuisine of her childhood and the modern, on-the-go cooking we do today. Brimming with irresistible recipes for meats, seafood, vegetables, noodles, and sweets, her latest book demystifies the multicooker and puts it to creative and inspiring use. It helps me bring Betty Ann's flavorful Filipino favorites to my weeknight and special occasion table with ease and delight.

Nancie McDermott, food writer, cooking teacher, cookbook author

---

Elizabeth Ann's new cookbook allows us to cook and taste authentic Filipino dishes right in our own kitchen. The mouthwatering recipes will also make you want to travel to the Philippines and experience its culture someday. For now, I really enjoy those classic dishes that would normally take hours to make with the help of Instant Pot™. Don't miss her famous Leche Flan recipe!

Namiko Chen, creator and recipe developer, Just One Cookbook

Betty Ann beautifully translates her mother's recipes for the modern cook, making them simple, approachable and fuss-free, thanks to convenient multicookers! Beloved recipes such as Pata Tim and Kare-Kare, which I fondly remember my own mother cooking in traditional pressure cookers, can now be made easily and are a must for every Filipino craving a taste of home.

Liren Legaspi Baker, creator of Kitchen Confidante

Praise & Accolades

Tita Betty Ann Besa-Quirino has honored our culture through food and recipes in her cookbook. She has sparked so much appreciation, respect and love for Filipino cooking and this cookbook honors the Filipino culture through food and recipes that are easily done at home for any home cook.

Johanna Marie Mirpuri, creator of Momma Cuisine, Media Personality, Executive Producer/Host #InTheKitch Show & live broadcast, founder of Figuri Media & ShopTheKitch.com

---

Elizabeth Ann Besa- Quirino, my dear friend and go-to expert for Filipino home cooking, has done it again! She presents a collection of Filipino favorites not only modified for American kitchens but also makes great use of the darling of American appliances, the Instant Pot™! Betty Ann's directions are clear, her recipes work, and now you'll be able to enjoy them while keeping your kitchen cool and your cleanup to a minimum. *Instant Filipino Recipes: My Mother's Traditional Philippine Food in a Multicooker Pot* is a wonderful companion to My Mother's Philippine Recipes, but it also stands on its own merit and will allow you to get the most out of your multicooker with tips on how long it will take to reach pressure, troubleshooting, and recipes from beverages to desserts!

Jenni Field, pastrychefonline.com, blogstamina.com

If you, like me, have always wanted to recreate your childhood comfort foods but balk at the time and energy required, then Elizabeth Ann Besa-Quirino's latest cookbook is for you! Betty Ann adapted her family's heirloom recipes for the American kitchen and further modified them for multicookers like the Instant Pot™. With *Instant Filipino Recipes: My Mother's Traditional Philippine Food in a Multicooker Pot*, you can recreate classic Pinoy recipes such as Arroz Caldo, Pancit Canton, Sinigang ng Baboy sa Bayabas, and Chicken Pastel in half the time but with all the flavor and soul of mom's cooking. Perfect for busy parents and working professionals!

Pat Tanumihardja, author of The Asian Grandmothers Cookbook and Farm to Table Asian Secrets—Vegan and Vegetarian Full-Flavored Recipes for Every Season

Table of Contents

Introduction

If you enjoy Filipino food but are looking for a faster, easier way to make home-cooked Filipino dishes, I can help.

Years after learning traditional Filipino cookery from my mother, I discovered I could now cook her Philippine recipes in half the time with my phenomenal Instant Pot®. But I was more than a little hesitant when I first invested in the multicooker nearly two years ago. While Mom was teaching me how to cook in her kitchen back in the Philippines, I was scared to use her pressure cooker. The 1960s-era contraption would whistle shrilly, blow out fiery steam and occasionally explode, sending its sealing valve ricocheting off the kitchen ceiling. I didn't tell my mother, but after seeing that, I vowed never to buy a pressure cooker when I grew up.

How things have changed. The new multicookers on the market today are practically everyone's best friend and are definitely not my mother's pressure cooker. There are currently many brands from which you can choose one that works best for your lifestyle and family. My personal choice was the Instant Pot® because of its user-friendly design and functionality. It can cook pretty much everything from soups and stews to beans and vegetables, and from porridge, pasta and rice to beef, poultry, pork and fish. My multicooker can cook on High Pressure or Low Pressure, from low to high, most of the time in less than 60 minutes. So, not only did I break my promise never to buy a multi-pressure cooker, I use mine daily. In fact, I bought several Instant Pots®. Some days, I use two at a time, and I am happiest when I can make soup and dessert simultaneously in under an hour for our weeknight family dinner.

What makes the Instant Pot® so special? Let me take you back to my childhood. When I was tall enough to reach the counter, my mother brought me into the kitchen to help her cook. I sat on a yellow bar stool that matched the sun-bright painted walls while I snipped the edges of the yardlong string beans my father grew in our backyard. My six-year-old self watched Mom as she stirred and tasted from the large cauldrons filled with different meats, seafood and vegetables bubbling and simmering on the stove. A large caldero of rice also had a special spot on the stovetop and would spew hot steam to signal when the fragrant kanin was ready.

My mother taught me the different methods in Philippine cookery: braising, boiling, steaming, pan-frying, sautéing and more. Tough cuts of meat, for instance, were tenderized after long hours on the stove or in clay pots over kindled firewood outdoors. As a child, I found such time-consuming and laborious methods rather daunting. I secretly doubted if I could ever manage to cook like Mom when I grew up.

Fast forward to the present day: as I write in my American kitchen, my Instant Pot® toils efficiently like a hands-free assistant chef. The multicooker can either cook on high pressure or function like a slow cooker; I simply toss in all the ingredients and walk away to do other things that need my attention. Best of all, I can cook classic Filipino recipes in less time than required with traditional methods. When my dishes come out of the Instant Pot®, the meats are tender and succulent, the seafood and fish are even more flavorful, the vegetables, noodles and rice are cooked in minutes, and traditional merienda and desserts are delightfully ready in half the time.

In this cookbook, I have put together a collection of my family's favorite Filipino recipes adapted for a multicooker like the Instant Pot®. You will find classic recipes such as Kare-Kare, Beef Pochero, Pata Tim, Tinolang Manok, Siomai, Adobong Pula, Mechado, Caldereta, Pancit Canton, Filipino Spaghetti, and Arroz Caldo, as well as fish and seafood, vegetables, noodles and rice. For a sweet finish, you can choose among snacks and desserts like Putong Puti, Kutchinta, Ube Haleya, Suman, Leche Flan, Banana-Mango Bread and a scintillating beverage of Pandan Iced Tea.

My choice of Philippine recipes to include was dictated by the amount of time needed to cook, such as meat cuts that require hours to tenderize. Like most of you, I've had to raise my children in a typical American suburban home. My sons' days were full with school and after-school sports and activities, while mine was packed as a working wife and mother. The most stressful hours for me were always before breakfast and after school when I needed to feed my children quickly or to make sure dinner was ready as soon as they got home. I cooked everything the traditional way back then. Today, I often think about how less stressed I would have been if the Instant Pot were around when I was raising children and juggling time between work and home.

Before you start cooking, it's important you read the user's manual that comes with the Instant Pot® or any multicooker appliance. Follow safety precautions and suggestions, and use cooking accessories recommended for multicookers, like only metal or silicone containers, which are sold online or at retail stores. The instructions in this cookbook are stated as clearly as possible for you to follow easily. After all, I am promising you a simpler way to cook Filipino food. To make it easy to follow the recipe, I've capitalized the first letter of the cooking functions—Sauté, Cancel, Manual, High Pressure, Steam, Keep Warm—and other buttons on the keypad.

I hope you will relish cooking Filipino food in the Instant Pot®, or any multicooker you choose, as much as I have. Always remember: life is not perfect, but with an Instant Pot to help put a scrumptious Filipino dinner on the table, it comes pretty close to it.

Sincerely,

Elizabeth Ann Besa-Quirino

Dedication

For my parents Lourdes Reyes and Gualberto Besa
For my husband Elpi and our sons Tim and Constante,
who have given me a multitude of reasons to cook with love.

What is a Multicooker?
Cook it Fast or Cook it Slow

A multicooker is a countertop kitchen appliance that gives you two options to cook: fast by way of high-pressure settings, like a pressure cooker, or slow, the way a slow cooker does.

Both options are convenient for most busy households. With the slow cooker setting, you can add all the ingredients to the multicooker before you leave for work and come home to dinner already made. High-pressure settings, on the other hand, are convenient for those hectic days when you have less than an hour to prepare dinner. Using either the high-pressure or slow-cooker methods, you'll have the advantage of hands-free, walk-away-from-it cooking that lets you do other things that need your attention. The multicooker is indeed a multitasker.

Today's various brands of multicookers, like the Instant Pot® I have in my kitchen, can make a difference in our cooking schedules and our lives. After all, most of us relish the thought of a delicious, home-cooked meal that is always ready in the least amount of time.

It was my desire to give you a quicker way to cook all-time Filipino favorite dishes just like I do in my American kitchen, so nearly all of the recipes in this cookbook use the high-pressure setting. Now, you can achieve the same flavors of a slow-cooked Filipino meal in half the time with these recipes using an Instant Pot® or similar types of multicooker.

Ways to Release the Pressure
with the Instant Pot®

Before you begin cooking with the Instant Pot® or any multicooker appliance, please read the product manual carefully. For your safety, follow all of the instructions and be mindful of the warnings.

When cooking with the Instant Pot®, there are three ways to release the pressure:

Quick Release is when you release the pressure instantly. Press *Cancel* and turn the *Steam* release handle on the lid to a *Venting* position.

Natural Release is when you press *Cancel* and wait for the pressure to come down on its own. When this happens, the lid unlocks. It takes about 20 minutes or may take a few minutes longer if the Instant Pot is full. Do not attempt to open the lid if it is still locked.

10-Minute Natural Release is when the pressure cooker goes into the *Keep Warm* mode by itself. Wait for 10 minutes when this happens. Then, press *Cancel* and turn the *Steam* release handle on the lid to a *Venting* position.

Appetizers & Soups

Binagis na Baka

Binagis na Baka

PROCEDURE

In a non-reactive mixing bowl, combine the ground beef and 2 tablespoons calamansi or lemon juice, and let the mixture marinate for 10 to 15 minutes.

Preheat the multicooker by selecting Sauté on high heat.

When the inside pot is heated, add the vegetable oil. Sauté the onions, garlic and scallions for 1 to 2 minutes.

Add the marinated ground beef and stir for 1 to 2 minutes. Click Cancel to turn off Sauté.

Pour the remaining ¼ cup calamansi or lemon juice, soy sauce and beef broth to the mixture.

Season with red pepper flakes, salt, ground black pepper and hot sauce. Do not stir.

Secure the lid. Check that the cooking pressure is on High and the release valve is set to Sealing.

Select High Pressure* for 7 minutes.

When cooking is complete, use a quick release. Carefully open the lid and stir the ingredients.

Serve warm. Garnish with chopped scallions, chilies and slices of calamansi or lemon.

*Note: After the initial Sauté, it takes about 17 to 20 minutes for the Instant Pot® to preheat before the High-Pressure cooking time begins. For other multicookers, please consult the product manual.

INGREDIENTS

1 pound ground beef

¼ cup plus 2 Tablespoons calamansi or lemon juice

2 Tablespoons vegetable oil

1 large red onion, sliced and divided—½ for sauté, ½ for garnish

2 garlic cloves, peeled and minced

2 scallion stalks, chopped and divided—½ for sauté, ½ for garnish

3 to 4 bird's eye chilies, sliced (plus additional chilies as desired for garnish)

1 Tablespoon soy sauce

½ cup beef broth

1 teaspoon red pepper flakes

1 teaspoon salt

1 teaspoon ground black pepper

½ teaspoon hot sauce

2 to 3 calamansi or 1 lemon, sliced

SERVINGS: 2 to 4
PREP TIME: 7 minutes
PRESSURE: 7 minutes
PRESSURE LEVEL: High. Release
CATEGORY: Quick

Pork Adobo Tacos

Pork Adobo Tacos

PROCEDURE

Marinate the pork with all of the ingredients except the chicken broth in a non-reactive bowl for 30 minutes.

Place the pork, including the marinade, and the chicken broth in the inside pot of the multicooker. Do not stir.

Secure the lid. Check that the cooking pressure is on High and the release valve is set to Sealing.

Select High Pressure* for 35 minutes.

When cooking is complete, use a quick release. Remove the pork. After 5 to 10 minutes, when the meat has cooled, shred the pork.

Assemble the tacos with the pork adobo filling and the topping ingredients as desired.

*Note: It takes about 17 to 20 minutes for the Instant Pot® to preheat before the High-Pressure cooking time begins. For other multicookers, please consult the product manual.

INGREDIENTS

1 pound pork belly or shoulder, cut into 2-inch cubes

½ cup cider vinegar

2 Tablespoons soy sauce

6 garlic cloves, peeled and minced

1 teaspoon whole black peppercorns

2 bay leaves

1 teaspoon salt

1 teaspoon ground black pepper

4 cups chicken broth

FOR TACOS & TOPPINGS

8 to 10 taco shells, hard or soft

3 tomatoes, chopped

1 large red or green bell pepper, chopped

2 large ripe mangoes, peeled, seeded and cubed

1 cup sour cream

1 cup mildly spicy salsa

2 cups shredded lettuce

1 to 2 cups grated cheddar cheese

SERVINGS: 4
PREP TIME: 30 minutes
PRESSURE: 35 minutes
PRESSURE LEVEL: High. Release
CATEGORY: Easy

Arroz Caldo

Arroz Caldo

PROCEDURE

Preheat the multicooker by selecting Sauté on high heat.

When the inside pot is heated (about 1 minute), add the vegetable oil. Sauté the garlic for about 2 minutes until crisp.

Remove the fried garlic and drain them on paper towels. Set aside.

Add the onions, ginger and scallions, and sauté.

Pour the patis into the pot and add the chicken pieces.

Scatter the rice grains over the chicken inside the pot.

Pour the water into the pot and season with salt and ground black pepper. Do not stir!

Secure the lid. Check that the cooking pressure is on High and the release valve is set to Sealing.

Select High Pressure* for 40 minutes.

Once cooking is complete, use a quick release. Open the lid carefully and stir the cooked rice and chicken, checking that none of the rice has stuck to the bottom.

Using a slotted spoon, remove the whole chicken pieces and transfer them to a large chopping board. Shred the meat into strips. Return the shredded chicken to the pot with the cooked rice and ginger broth.

Serve warm. Garnish with slices of calamansi or lemon, hard-boiled eggs, scallions and the crisp garlic.

*Note: After the initial Sauté, it takes about 17 to 20 minutes for the Instant Pot® to preheat before the High-Pressure cooking time begins. For other multicookers, please consult the product manual.

INGREDIENTS

2 Tablespoons vegetable oil

6 garlic cloves, peeled and minced

1 large white or yellow onion, chopped

1-inch knob fresh ginger, peeled and sliced thinly

2 scallion stalks, sliced diagonally and divided; use white parts for sauté, greens for garnish

2 Tablespoons patis (fish sauce)

½ pound bone-in chicken thighs (about 3 pieces)

1 cup uncooked white rice

8 to 10 cups water

1 teaspoon salt

1 teaspoon ground black pepper

2 to 4 calamansi or 1 large lemon, sliced

2 hard-boiled eggs, peeled and sliced

SERVINGS: 4 to 6
PREP TIME: 10 minutes
PRESSURE: 40 minutes
PRESSURE LEVEL: High. Release
CATEGORY: Easy

Manila Clam Soup with Spinach

Manila Clam Soup with Spinach

PROCEDURE

Soak live clams in a large bowl of water and wash thoroughly. Set aside.

Preheat the multicooker by selecting Sauté on high heat.

When the inside pot is heated (about 1 minute), add the vegetable oil. Then, as the oil heats up, add the butter.

Sauté the garlic, onions and ginger.

Add the patis. Click Cancel to turn off the Sauté.

Toss in the clams. Pour in the white wine and broth, and season with salt and black pepper.

Secure the lid. Check that the cooking pressure is on High and the release valve is set to Sealing.

Select Manual and cook at High Pressure* for 8 minutes.

When cooking is complete, use a quick release and carefully open the lid.

While the broth is bubbling hot, add the spinach and stir to mix.

Close the lid. Click Keep Warm for 5 minutes to cook the greens. Click Cancel to turn off.

Serve the soup warm and garnished with scallions.

*Note: It takes about 17 to 20 minutes for the Instant Pot® to preheat before the High-Pressure cooking time begins. For other multicookers, please consult the product manual.

INGREDIENTS

1 ½ pounds live Manila clams (or substitute mussels)

2 Tablespoons vegetable oil

2 Tablespoons unsalted butter

4 garlic cloves, peeled and minced

1 large white or yellow onion, chopped

1-inch knob fresh ginger, peeled and sliced thinly

1 Tablespoon patis (fish sauce)

2 Tablespoons white wine

6 to 8 cups vegetable broth

1 teaspoon salt

1 teaspoon ground black pepper

2 to 3 cups fresh spinach leaves, stems trimmed, or substitute malunggay (moringa)

1 to 2 scallion stalks, chopped

SERVINGS: 4
PREP TIME: 10 minutes
PRESSURE: 8 minutes
PRESSURE LEVEL: High. Release
CATEGORY: Easy

Sabaw ng Tinolang Manok

Sabaw ng Tinolang Manok

PROCEDURE

Preheat the multicooker by selecting Sauté on high heat.

When the inside pot is heated (about 1 minute), add the vegetable oil.

Sauté the garlic, onions and ginger for 1 to 2 minutes. Add the patis.

Click Cancel to turn off the Sauté button.

Add the chicken pieces, broth and chayote. Season with black peppercorns, salt and ground black pepper.

Secure lid. Check that the cooking pressure is on High and the release valve is set to Sealing.

Select High Pressure* and cook for 40 minutes.

When cooking is complete, use a quick release. Carefully open the lid and stir the ingredients.

Add the fresh spinach or malunggay leaves.

Close the lid. Click Keep Warm to cook spinach or malunggay for 5 minutes.

Serve warm.

*Note: It takes about 17 to 20 minutes for the Instant Pot® to preheat before the High-Pressure cooking time begins. For other multicookers, please consult the product manual.

INGREDIENTS

2 Tablespoons vegetable oil

2 garlic cloves, peeled and minced

1 large white or yellow onion, chopped

1-inch knob fresh ginger, peeled and sliced

2 Tablespoons patis (fish sauce)

4 pounds bone-in chicken, cut up (about 6 to 8 pieces)

8 to 10 cups organic chicken broth

1 chayote, peeled and quartered

1 teaspoon whole black peppercorns

1 teaspoon salt

1 teaspoon ground black pepper

2 cups fresh spinach or malunggay (moringa) leaves

SERVINGS: 4
PREP TIME: 10 minutes
PRESSURE: 40 minutes
PRESSURE LEVEL: High. Release
CATEGORY: Easy

Sotanghon Soup with Bola-Bola

Sotanghon Soup with Bola-Bola

PROCEDURE

Soak the sotanghon noodles in a bowl of room temperature water for 15 to 20 minutes. Drain the water and set the noodles aside.

In a large bowl, combine the ground beef, half of the onions, egg, rice wine, soy sauce, breadcrumbs, flour, salt and ground black pepper. Mix well. Shape a tablespoon of the mixture into 1-inch meatballs (bola-bola). Refrigerate for 10 minutes.

Preheat the multicooker by selecting Sauté on high heat.

When the inside pot is heated (about 1 minute), add the vegetable oil. Sauté the remaining onions, garlic and celery for 1 to 2 minutes. Click Cancel to turn off the Sauté button.

Add the patis and broth, and then add the meatballs to the broth.

Secure the lid. Check that the cooking pressure is on High and the release valve is set to Sealing.

Select Manual and cook at High Pressure* for 12 minutes.

When cooking is complete, use a quick release and carefully open the lid.

Add the sotanghon noodles and the snow peas. Stir the ingredients.

Close the lid. Click Keep Warm for 5 minutes for the noodles and vegetables to cook in the residual heat.

Serve warm and garnished with scallions.

*Note: It takes about 17 to 20 minutes for the Instant Pot® to preheat before the High-Pressure cooking time begins. For other multicookers, please consult the product manual.

Cook's comments: Ground pork can be substituted for beef in the same amount indicated.

INGREDIENTS

8 ounces dried sotanghon (cellophane) noodles

1 pound ground beef

2 large white or yellow onions, chopped and divided—½ for meatballs, ½ for sautéing

1 egg

1 Tablespoon Shaoxing rice wine

1 Tablespoon soy sauce

¼ cup bread crumbs

1 Tablespoon all-purpose flour

1 teaspoon salt

1 teaspoon ground black pepper

2 Tablespoons vegetable oil

2 garlic cloves, peeled and minced

1 cup chopped celery

1 Tablespoon patis (fish sauce)

6 to 8 cups organic vegetable or beef broth

2 cups snow peas, edges trimmed

1 to 2 scallion stalks, chopped

SERVINGS: 4
PREP TIME: 30 minutes
PRESSURE: 12 minutes
PRESSURE LEVEL: High. Release
CATEGORY: Easy

Rice & Noodles

Filipino Spaghetti with Meat Sauce

Filipino Spaghetti with Meat Sauce

PROCEDURE

Preheat the multicooker by selecting Sauté on high heat.

When the inside pot is heated (about 1 minute), add the vegetable oil. Sauté the garlic and onions for 1 to 2 minutes.

Add the ground beef to the sauté and stir for about 2 to 3 minutes as the meat browns.

Click Cancel to turn off Sauté.

Level off the ground beef so that it is spread evenly in the bottom of the pot.

Layer the following ingredients in order, from bottom to top: uncooked pasta, tomato sauce, tomato paste, crushed tomatoes and ketchup.

Sprinkle brown sugar, salt and black pepper on top of the sauces.

Pour the water along the sides of the pot. Do not pour directly on top of the pasta or tomato sauces as it will dislodge the noodles and they won't cook evenly. Do not stir!

Secure the lid. Check that the cooking pressure is on High and that the release valve is set to Sealing.

Select Manual and cook at High Pressure* for 7 minutes.

Once cooking is complete, use a quick release. Test if the pasta is cooked. If it is not yet done, select Sauté and, keeping the lid open, simmer for another 1 to 2 minutes.

Serve spaghetti topped with freshly grated Parmesan cheese.

*Note: After the initial Sauté, it takes about 17 to 20 minutes for the Instant Pot® to preheat before the High-Pressure cooking time begins. For other multicookers, please consult the product manual.

INGREDIENTS

2 Tablespoons vegetable oil

4 garlic cloves, peeled and minced

1 large onion, chopped

1 pound ground beef

1 pound uncooked spaghetti, broken in half or thirds

1 (15-ounce) can tomato sauce

1 (6-ounce) can tomato paste

1 (6-ounce) can crushed tomatoes

1 cup banana ketchup

1 Tablespoon brown sugar

1 teaspoon salt

1 teaspoon ground black pepper

4 cups water

1 cup freshly grated Parmesan cheese

SERVINGS: 4
PREP TIME: 10 minutes
PRESSURE: 7 minutes
PRESSURE LEVEL: High. Release
CATEGORY: Quick

Pancit Canton

Pancit Canton

PROCEDURE

Preheat the multicooker by selecting Sauté on high heat.

When the inside pot is heated (about 1 minute), add the vegetable oil. As soon as the oil is hot, add the Chinese sausages and stir-fry for 1 to 2 minutes or until the edges are crisp. Remove the sausages from the pot and drain on paper towels. Set aside.

While Sauté is on, add the garlic, onions, celery and half of the chopped scallions. Sauté for 1 to 2 minutes.

Add the pork and shrimp. Sauté for 2 minutes.

Turn off the Sauté button by clicking Cancel.

Level off the ingredients so that they are flat as you start adding the remaining ingredients in layers.

Pour the calamansi and soy sauce over the sautéed mixture.

Add the carrots and green beans.

Place the dried pancit canton noodles on top of the vegetables. Arrange the dry noodles in an even, flat layer over the vegetables and meat. Season with salt and ground black pepper.

Pour the broth along the side of the pot, making sure not to dislodge the noodles. Do not stir!

(continued on next page)

INGREDIENTS

2 Tablespoons vegetable oil

2 Chinese sausages, sliced (about ½ cup)

2 garlic cloves, peeled and minced

1 large onion, chopped

1 cup chopped celery

2 scallion stalks, chopped and divided—½ for sautéing, ½ for garnish

½ pound pork shoulder, sliced into 2-inch strips

¼ pound large shrimp, peeled with heads and tails removed

1 Tablespoon calamansi or lemon juice

2 Tablespoons low-sodium soy sauce

1 medium carrot, peeled and sliced

1 cup sliced green beans (2-inch pieces)

12 ounces dried pancit canton noodles

½ teaspoon salt

1 teaspoon ground black pepper

1 ½ cups vegetable broth

2 to 3 calamansi or 1 lemon, sliced

SERVINGS: 4
PREP TIME: 10 minutes
PRESSURE: 7 minutes
PRESSURE LEVEL: High. Release
CATEGORY: Quick

Pancit Canton

PROCEDURE

(continued from previous page)

Secure the lid. Check that the cooking pressure is on High and the release valve is set to Sealing.

Select Manual and cook at High Pressure* for 7 minutes.

When cooking is complete, use a quick release before opening lid.

Stir the ingredients. Add the Chinese sausages on top of the pancit canton.

Serve warm, garnished with the remaining scallions and slices of calamansi or lemon.

*Note: It takes about 17 to 20 minutes for the Instant Pot® to preheat before the High-Pressure cooking time begins. For other multicookers, please consult the product manual.

Cook's comments: Use sliced chicken or beef sirloin strips in place of the pork, if preferred.

33

Pandan Rice

Pandan Rice

PROCEDURE

Wash the rice grains with water twice. Discard water and set the rice aside.

Pour the vegetable oil into the inside pot. Tilt the pot to spread the oil.

Line the bottom of the pot with 3 pandan leaves.

Add the rice, water and salt.

Place the remaining pandan leaves on top.

Secure the lid. Check that the cooking pressure is on High and the release valve is set to Sealing.

Select Rice on key pad at Low Pressure* for 12 minutes.

When cooking is complete, use a quick release and carefully open the lid.

Fluff the rice with a fork. Serve warm as an accompaniment.

*Note: It takes about 17 to 20 minutes for the Instant Pot® to preheat before the Pressure cooking time begins. For other multicookers, please consult the product manual.

INGREDIENTS

1 ½ cups uncooked jasmine or any long grain white rice

1 teaspoon vegetable oil

6 fresh or frozen pandan leaves

1 ½ cups water

1 teaspoon salt

SERVINGS: 2
PREP TIME: 7 minutes
PRESSURE: 12 minutes
PRESSURE LEVEL: Low. Rice.
CATEGORY: Easy

Vegetables

Adobong Talong at Ampalaya

Adobong Talong at Ampalaya

PROCEDURE

Preheat the multicooker by selecting Sauté on high heat.

When the inside pot is heated (about 1 minute), add the vegetable oil. Sauté the garlic and onions for 1 to 2 minutes. Click Cancel to turn off Sauté.

Add the bagoong guisado, eggplants and ampalaya.

Pour the vinegar and vegetable broth into the pot. Add the black peppercorns and bay leaves, and season with salt and ground black pepper.

Secure the lid. Check that the cooking pressure is on High and the release valve is set to Sealing.

Select High Pressure–Vegetables* and cook for 5 minutes.

When cooking is complete, use a quick release and carefully open the lid.

Add the brown sugar and stir all of the ingredients.

Close the lid. Select Keep Warm for 2 minutes so that the sugar can blend with the flavors. Serve immediately while warm.

*Note: After the initial Sauté, it takes about 17 to 20 minutes for the Instant Pot® to preheat before the High-Pressure cooking time begins. For other multicookers, please consult the product manual.

INGREDIENTS

2 Tablespoons vegetable oil

6 garlic cloves, peeled and minced

1 large onion, sliced

1 Tablespoon bagoong guisado (sautéed shrimp paste) – see Glossary

2 cups sliced Asian eggplants

2 ampalaya (bitter melon), seeded and sliced

½ cup cider vinegar

2 cups organic vegetable broth

1 teaspoon whole black peppercorns

2 bay leaves

½ teaspoon salt

1 teaspoon ground black pepper

1 teaspoon brown sugar

SERVINGS: 4
PREP TIME: 10 minutes
PRESSURE: 5 minutes
PRESSURE LEVEL: High. Release
CATEGORY: Easy

Chop Suey with Casuy

Chop Suey with Casuy

PROCEDURE

Prepare the multicooker by selecting Sauté on high heat.

When the inside pot is heated (about 1 minute), add the vegetable oil. Sauté the garlic, onions and celery for 1 to 2 minutes.

Add the chicken and oyster sauce. Stir for about 2 to 3 minutes as the meat browns.

Click Cancel to turn off Sauté.

Add the carrots, broccoli, green beans and bell peppers.

Pour the broth into the pot and season with salt and black pepper.

Secure the lid. Check that the cooking pressure is on High and the release valve is set to Sealing.

Select Manual and cook at High Pressure* for 7 minutes.

When cooking is complete, use a quick release and carefully open the lid.

Add the shredded cabbage and the casuy.

Click Keep Warm for 5 minutes so that the cabbage cooks in the residual heat. Click Cancel to turn off.

Serve warm garnished with chopped scallions.

*Note: It takes about 17 to 20 minutes for the Instant Pot® to preheat before the High-Pressure cooking time begins. For other multicookers, please consult the product manual.

INGREDIENTS

2 Tablespoons vegetable oil

2 garlic cloves, peeled and minced

1 white or yellow onion, sliced

½ cup chopped celery

½ pound boneless chicken breasts, sliced into 2-inch strips

2 Tablespoons oyster sauce

1 medium carrot, peeled and sliced

2 cups broccoli florets

2 cups sliced green beans (2-inch pieces)

1 red or green bell pepper, seeded and sliced

2 cups vegetable or chicken broth

1 teaspoon salt

1 teaspoon ground black pepper

2 cups shredded cabbage

½ cup casuy (cashew nuts)

1 to 2 scallion stalks, chopped

SERVINGS: 4
PREP TIME: 15 minutes
PRESSURE: 7 minutes
PRESSURE LEVEL: High. Release
CATEGORY: Easy

Guinataang Sitaw at Kalabasa

Guinataang Sitaw at Kalabasa

PROCEDURE

Preheat the multicooker by selecting Sauté on high heat.

When the inside pot is heated (about 1 minute), add the vegetable oil. Sauté the garlic, onions and ginger for 1 to 2 minutes. Add the patis.

Click Cancel to turn off the Sauté button.

Add the sitaw and kalabasa. Pour the vegetable broth into the pot. Season with salt and black pepper.

Secure the lid. Check that the cooking pressure is on High and the release valve is set to Sealing.

Select High Pressure* and cook for 8 minutes.

When cooking is complete, use a quick release and carefully open the lid.

Pour the coconut milk into the pot and stir the ingredients together.

Close the lid. Click Keep Warm for 8 minutes for the flavors to blend.

Serve warm with steamed rice.

*Note: After the initial Sauté, it takes about 17 to 20 minutes for the Instant Pot® to preheat before the High-Pressure cooking time begins. For other multicookers, please consult the product manual.

INGREDIENTS

2 Tablespoons vegetable oil

2 garlic cloves, peeled and minced

1 large white or yellow onion, sliced

1-inch knob fresh ginger, peeled and sliced

2 Tablespoons patis (fish sauce)

2 cups sliced sitaw (long green beans), cut into 2-inch pieces

3 cups cubed kalabasa (kabocha squash), cut into 2-inch cubes

2 cups organic vegetable broth

1 teaspoon salt

1 teaspoon ground black pepper

1 (15-ounce) can coconut milk

SERVINGS: 4
PREP TIME: 15 minutes
PRESSURE: 8 minutes
PRESSURE LEVEL: High. Release
CATEGORY: Quick

Inabraw na Hipon at Gulay

Inabraw na Hipon at Gulay

PROCEDURE

In the inner pot, layer the following ingredients in order, from bottom to top: shrimps, eggplants, ampalaya, okra, tomatoes, sitaw, garlic, onions and ginger.

Add the broth or water and season with the bagoong guisado, salt and ground black pepper.

Secure the lid. Check that the cooking pressure is on High and the release valve is set to Sealing.

Select Manual and cook at High Pressure* for 8 minutes.

When cooking is complete, use a quick release and carefully open the lid.

Add the malunggay leaves and stir the mixture.

Click Keep Warm for 5 minutes for the malunggay to cook in the residual heat. Click Cancel to turn off.

Serve warm with a side of steamed rice.

*Note: It takes about 17 to 20 minutes for the Instant Pot® to preheat before the High-Pressure cooking time begins. For other multicookers, please consult the product manual.

INGREDIENTS

½ pound fresh shrimp, peeled with heads and tails removed

2 Asian eggplants, sliced

1 ampalaya (bitter melon), seeded and sliced

6 to 8 okra

2 medium tomatoes, quartered

2 cups sitaw (long green beans) sliced into 2-inch pieces

2 garlic cloves, peeled and minced

1 large onion, sliced

1-inch knob fresh ginger, peeled

3 to 4 cups vegetable broth or water

1 Tablespoon bagoong guisado (sautéed shrimp paste) – see Glossary

½ teaspoon salt

1 teaspoon ground black pepper

1 to 2 cups malunggay (moringa) leaves, fresh or frozen

Steamed rice

SERVINGS: 2 to 4
PREP TIME: 10 minutes
PRESSURE: 8 minutes
PRESSURE LEVEL: High. Release
CATEGORY: Easy

Monggo Guisado

Monggo Guisado

PROCEDURE

Soak the monggo in a bowl of water for 30 minutes. Drain and discard the water. Set the beans aside.

Preheat the multicooker by selecting Sauté on high heat.

When the inside pot is heated (about 1 minute), add the vegetable oil. Sauté the garlic, onions, ginger and tomatoes for 1 to 2 minutes. Add the patis to the sauté.

Click Cancel to turn off Sauté.

Combine the monggo and vegetable broth in the multicooker and season with salt and black pepper.

Secure the lid. Check that the cooking pressure is on High and the release valve is set to Sealing.

Select Manual and cook at High Pressure* for 15 minutes. When cooking is complete, use a quick release and carefully open the lid.

Stir the monggo mixture and then add the fresh spinach.

Close the lid. Press Keep Warm for 5 minutes for the spinach to cook in the residual heat.

Serve warm with steamed rice.

*Note: It takes about 17 to 20 minutes for the Instant Pot® to preheat before the High-Pressure cooking time begins. For other multicookers, please consult the product manual.

INGREDIENTS

1 cup dried monggo (mung beans)

2 Tablespoons vegetable oil

2 garlic cloves, peeled and minced

1 large white or yellow onion, chopped

1-inch knob fresh ginger, peeled and sliced

1 large tomato, halved then sliced

1 Tablespoon *patis* (fish sauce)

3 to 4 cups organic vegetable broth

½ teaspoon salt

1 teaspoon ground black pepper

2 cups fresh spinach

SERVINGS: 4
PREP TIME: 30 minutes
PRESSURE: 15 minutes
PRESSURE LEVEL: High. Release
CATEGORY: Easy

Fish & Seafood

Alimango sa Gata

Alimango sa Gata

PROCEDURE

Preheat the multicooker by selecting Sauté on high heat.

When the inside pot is heated (about 1 minute), add the vegetable oil.

Sauté the garlic, onions, ginger, patis and tomatoes.

Click Cancel to turn off the Sauté button.

Add the steamed crabs, chilies and peppers.

Pour the broth into the pot and season with salt and ground black pepper.

Secure the lid. Check that the cooking pressure is on High and the release valve is set to Sealing.

Select Manual and cook at High Pressure* for 8 minutes.

When cooking is complete, use a quick release and carefully open the lid.

Pour the coconut cream into the pot and stir the ingredients.

Close the lid. Click Keep Warm for 7 minutes so that the coconut cream blends with the crabs and other ingredients. Click Cancel to turn off.

Serve warm, garnished with scallions.

*Note: After the initial Sauté, it takes about 17 to 20 minutes for the Instant Pot® to preheat before the High-Pressure cooking time begins. For other multicookers, please consult the product manual.

Cook's Comment: This recipe uses pre-steamed crabs. Some fishmongers will steam crabs and lobsters by customer request for free; take advantage of this offer. If you prefer, bring home live crabs in season and soak them in water to remove the grime and dirt. Then, steam the crabs on the stovetop for 10 minutes before adding them to the recipe.

INGREDIENTS

2 Tablespoons vegetable oil

2 garlic cloves, peeled and minced

1 large white or yellow onion, chopped

1-inch knob fresh ginger, peeled and sliced

1 teaspoon patis (fish sauce)

2 large tomatoes, sliced crosswise

2 pounds freshly steamed whole crabs (about 2 to 3 large pieces) - see Cook's comment

1 to 2 bird's eye chilies

1 to 2 siling mahaba (mild, finger-like peppers)

4 cups vegetable broth

1 teaspoon salt

1 teaspoon ground black pepper

1 (15-ounce) can coconut cream

1 to 2 scallion stalks, chopped

SERVINGS: 2 to 4
PREP TIME: 10 minutes
PRESSURE: 8 minutes
PRESSURE LEVEL: High. Release
CATEGORY: Easy

Fish Fillets with Black Beans and Tofu

Fish Fillets with Black Beans and Tofu

PROCEDURE

Soak the salted black beans in a small bowl of water for 20 minutes to soften.

In a medium non-reactive bowl, marinate the fish in calamansi or lemon juice, salt and black pepper for 15 minutes in the refrigerator.

Preheat the multicooker by selecting Sauté on high heat.

When the inside pot is heated (about 1 minute), add the vegetable oil. Sauté the garlic, onions and ginger. Click Cancel to turn off Sauté.

Place the fish fillets and the marinade in the pot. Add the black beans on top of the fish.

Pour in the oyster sauce and vegetable broth.

Secure the lid. Check that the cooking pressure is on High and the release valve is set to Sealing.

Select Manual and cook at High Pressure* for 7 minutes.

When cooking is complete, use a quick release and carefully open the lid.

Add the sugar and stir gently.

Add the snow peas and tofu over the fish.

Close the lid. Click Keep Warm for 5 minutes to cook the snow peas in the residual heat.

Click Cancel to turn off.

Serve warm garnished with scallions.

*Note: After the initial Sauté, it takes about 17 to 20 minutes for the Instant Pot® to preheat before the High-Pressure cooking time begins. For other multicookers, please consult the product manual.

INGREDIENTS

½ cup Chinese salted black beans, drained

1 pound tilapia fillets (or any white fish)

1 Tablespoon calamansi or lemon juice

1 teaspoon salt

1 teaspoon ground black pepper

2 Tablespoons vegetable oil

2 garlic cloves, peeled and minced

1 large white or yellow onion, sliced

1-inch knob fresh ginger, peeled and sliced

2 Tablespoons oyster sauce

4 cups vegetable broth

1 teaspoon brown sugar

1 to 2 cups snow peas, edges trimmed

1 whole (16-ounce) extra-firm tofu, cut into 2-inch cubes

1 to 2 scallion stalks, chopped for garnish

SERVINGS: 2 to 4
PREP TIME: 30 minutes
PRESSURE: 7 minutes
PRESSURE LEVEL: High. Release
CATEGORY: Quick

Nilasing na Hipon

Nilasing na Hipon

PROCEDURE

Wash the shrimp thoroughly. Discard the water.

Place the shrimp, broth, wine, garlic, onions, salt and black pepper in the inside pot.

Secure the lid. Check that the cooking pressure is on High and the release valve is set to Sealing.

Select High Pressure* – Steam for 8 minutes.

When cooking is complete, use a quick release and carefully open the lid. Drain and discard the liquid.

Serve the shrimp garnished with scallions and sliced calamansi or lemon.

*Note: It takes about 17 to 20 minutes for the Instant Pot® to preheat before the High-Pressure cooking time begins. For other multicookers, please consult the product manual.

Cook's comments: Save the shrimp heads to make seafood stock for other dishes.

INGREDIENTS

2 pounds large shrimp, peeled with heads and tails removed

2 cups organic vegetable broth

¼ cup white wine

6 garlic cloves, peeled and minced

1 large white or yellow onion, sliced

1 teaspoon salt

1 teaspoon ground black pepper

2 scallion stalks, chopped

2 to 3 calamansi or 1 lemon, sliced

SERVINGS: 4
PREP TIME: 7 minutes
PRESSURE: 8 minutes
PRESSURE LEVEL: High. Steam.
CATEGORY: Quick

Paksiw na Isda

Paksiw na Isda

PROCEDURE

In the inside pot, layer the following ingredients in order, from bottom to top: fish, ginger, garlic, onions and siling mahaba.

Scatter the ampalaya slices over the fish.

Pour the vinegar, patis and water into the pot and season with black peppercorns and salt.

Secure the lid. Check that the cooking pressure is on High and the release valve is set to Sealing.

Select Manual and cook at High Pressure* for 10 minutes.

When cooking is complete, use a quick release and carefully open the lid.

Gently stir the ingredients to combine. Serve the fish with the broth in a deep dish.

*Note: It takes about 17 to 20 minutes for the Instant Pot® to preheat before the High-Pressure cooking time begins. For other multicookers, please consult the product manual.

Cook's comments: If using whole fish, ask the fishmonger to remove the scales, intestines and gills, and to cut off the tail and head if you prefer.

INGREDIENTS

1 pound white fish such as bangus (milkfish), tilapia, pompano or snapper, whole or filleted

1-inch knob fresh ginger, peeled and sliced

4 garlic cloves, peeled and minced

1 large white or yellow onion, sliced

2 siling mahaba (mild, finger-like peppers)

1 ampalaya (bitter melon), seeded and sliced

½ cup white vinegar

1 Tablespoon patis (fish sauce)

3 to 4 cups water

1 Tablespoon whole black peppercorns

1 teaspoon salt

SERVINGS: 2 to 4
PREP TIME: 10 minutes
PRESSURE: 10 minutes
PRESSURE LEVEL: High. Release
CATEGORY: Quick

Meats

Adobong Pula with Pineapple

Adobong Pula with Pineapple

PROCEDURE

In a small bowl, soak the achuete seeds in warm water for 15 minutes. When the water turns slightly red, pour the seeds and water through a sieve, pressing down on the seeds. Save about ½ cup of the reddish liquid and discard the seeds.

Combine the vinegar, garlic, salt, black peppercorns, bay leaves and ground black pepper, and marinate the chicken in the mixture for 15 to 20 minutes.

Preheat the multicooker by selecting Sauté on high heat.

When the inside pot is heated (about 1 minute), add the vegetable oil. Add the chicken pieces and brown for about 2 to 3 minutes. Click Cancel to turn off the Sauté button.

Add the chicken and marinade to the pot.

Pour in the achuete liquid and the chicken broth.

Secure the lid. Check that the cooking pressure is on High and the release valve is set to Sealing.

Select High Pressure* and cook for 40 minutes.

When cooking is complete, use a quick release. Carefully open the lid and stir the ingredients.

Add the pineapple chunks. Close the lid. Select Keep Warm for 5 minutes for the pineapple to blend with the adobo flavors. Serve warm.

*Note: After the initial Sauté, it takes about 17 to 20 minutes for the Instant Pot® to preheat before the High-Pressure cooking time begins. For other multicookers, please consult the product manual.

Cook's comment: Be mindful that achuete can stain your skin, fabrics, utensils and kitchenware

INGREDIENTS

1 Tablespoon achuete seeds

1 cup warm water

4 pounds chicken, bone-in and cut into serving pieces (about 6 to 8 pieces)

½ cup cider vinegar

6 cloves garlic, peeled and minced

½ Tablespoon salt

1 teaspoon whole black peppercorns

2 bay leaves

1 teaspoon ground black pepper

2 Tablespoons vegetable oil

6 cups organic chicken broth

1 cup pineapple chunks

SERVINGS: 4
PREP TIME: 20 minutes
PRESSURE: 40 minutes
PRESSURE LEVEL: High. Release
CATEGORY: Easy

Beef Mechado

Beef Mechado

PROCEDURE

Place the whole beef roast in a large mixing bowl and pierce all over with a fork. Marinate with the calamansi or lemon juice and soy sauce for 30 minutes.

Preheat the multicooker by selecting Sauté on high heat. When the inside pot is heated (about 1 minute), add the vegetable oil. Brown the roast on all sides for 2 to 3 minutes.

Add the garlic, onions, bell peppers, tomatoes and potatoes. Sauté for 2 to 3 minutes. Click Cancel to turn off the Sauté button.

Add the tomato paste and pour in the broth. Season with salt and ground black pepper.

Secure the lid. Check that the cooking pressure is on High and the release valve is set to Sealing.

Select High Pressure* and cook for 45 minutes.

When cooking is complete, use a quick release and carefully open the lid.

After the meat has rested for about 10 minutes, remove it from the pot and slice into serving pieces. Arrange on a platter. Pour the broth over the beef and garnish with chopped parsley.

*Note: After the initial Sauté, it takes about 17 to 20 minutes for the Instant Pot® to preheat before the High-Pressure cooking time begins. For other multicookers, please consult the product manual.

INGREDIENTS

4 pounds whole beef chuck roast

1 Tablespoon calamansi or lemon juice

¼ cup soy sauce

2 Tablespoons vegetable oil

2 garlic cloves, peeled and minced

1 large white or yellow onion, sliced

1 red or green bell pepper, seeded and sliced

¼ pound tomatoes (about 4), quartered

2 medium potatoes, peeled and quartered

1 medium carrot, peeled and sliced

1 (6-ounce) can tomato paste

6 to 8 cups organic beef broth

1 teaspoon salt

1 teaspoon ground black pepper

2 Tablespoons chopped fresh parsley

SERVINGS: 4 to 6
PREP TIME: 30 minutes
PRESSURE: 45 minutes
PRESSURE LEVEL: High. Pressure.
CATEGORY: Moderately Easy

Beef Caldereta

Beef Caldereta

PROCEDURE

Preheat the multicooker by selecting Sauté on high heat.

When the inside pot is heated (about 1 minute), add the extra virgin olive oil and butter. Braise the beef short ribs for 5 minutes, turning them over to brown on all sides. Sprinkle the Worcestershire sauce over the ribs.

Add the garlic, onions and bell peppers. Continue sautéing for 1 to 2 minutes.

Click Cancel to turn off the Sauté button.

Add the tomato paste and liver spread. Pour the beef broth into the pot.

Add the potatoes and olives. Season with red pepper flakes, salt and ground black pepper.

Secure the lid. Check that the cooking pressure is on High and the release valve is set to Sealing.

Select High Pressure* for 45 minutes.

When cooking is complete, use a quick release. Open the lid carefully.

Serve warm with steamed rice.

*Note: After the initial Sauté, it takes about 17 to 20 minutes for the Instant Pot® to preheat before the High-Pressure cooking time begins. For other multicookers, please consult the product manual.

INGREDIENTS

2 Tablespoons extra virgin olive oil

2 Tablespoons unsalted butter

4 pounds beef short ribs, about 5 to 6 pieces

1 Tablespoon Worcestershire sauce

4 garlic cloves, peeled and minced

1 large white or yellow onion, chopped

1 whole red or green bell pepper, seeded and sliced

1 (6-ounce) can tomato paste

½ cup canned liver spread

6 cups beef broth

3 medium potatoes, peeled and quartered

½ cup pitted Spanish green olives with pimiento

1 teaspoon red pepper flakes

1 teaspoon salt

1 teaspoon ground black pepper

SERVINGS: 4
PREP TIME: 10 minutes
PRESSURE: 45 minutes
PRESSURE LEVEL: High. Pressure
CATEGORY: Easy

Chicken and Beef Pochero with Vegetables

Chicken and Beef Pochero with Vegetables

PROCEDURE

Preheat the multicooker by selecting Sauté on high heat.

When the inside pot is heated (about 1 minute), add the vegetable oil. Heat for 1 minute and add the sliced plantains to brown. Turn and cook the pieces for 2 to 3 minutes. Remove the plantains from the pot and drain on paper towels. Set aside.

Add the chorizos to the pot and stir-fry for 2 minutes until slightly browned. Remove the chorizos from the pot and drain on paper towels. Set aside.

Add the beef and chicken to the inside pot. Stir-fry for 2 minutes until the meat is browned.

Sauté the garlic and onions. Add the patis.

Click Cancel to turn off the Sauté button.

Add the potatoes and carrots to the mix. Pour the tomato sauce and broth into the pot and season with salt and black pepper. Do not stir.

Secure the lid. Check that the cooking pressure is on High and the release valve is set to Sealing.

Select High Pressure* and cook for 45 minutes.

When cooking is complete, use a quick release and carefully open the lid.

(continued on next page)

INGREDIENTS

4 Tablespoons vegetable oil

2 large plantains, peeled and sliced diagonally into 2-inch pieces

2 Spanish chorizos, sliced

2 pounds beef stew meat, cut into 2-inch cubes

2 pounds bone-in chicken, cut into serving pieces

4 garlic cloves, peeled and minced

1 large white onion, chopped

1 Tablespoon *patis* (fish sauce)

2 medium potatoes, peeled and quartered

1 medium carrot, peeled and sliced

1 (15-ounce) can tomato sauce

6 to 8 cups organic chicken or beef broth

1 teaspoon salt

1 teaspoon ground black pepper

1 Tablespoon brown sugar

1 cup sliced green beans (2-inch pieces)

2 cups shredded cabbage

SERVINGS: 4 to 6
PREP TIME: 30 minutes
PRESSURE: 45 minutes
PRESSURE LEVEL: High. Release.
CATEGORY: Moderately Easy

Chicken and Beef Pochero with Vegetables

PROCEDURE *(continued from previous page)*

Add the brown sugar. Return the chorizos to the pot. Stir the ingredients.

Add the green beans and cabbage while the sauce is bubbling hot.

Close the lid. Click Keep Warm for 7 minutes so that the vegetables are cooked.

Plate the meats nestled with the vegetables on a large platter. Serve the tomato sauce broth on the side. Serve this dish paired with the plantains.

Note: It takes about 17 to 20 minutes for the Instant Pot® to preheat before the High-Pressure cooking time begins. For other multicookers, please consult the product manual.

Chicken Pastel

Chicken Pastel

PROCEDURE

Preheat the multicooker by selecting Sauté on high heat.

When the inside pot is heated (about 1 minute), add the extra virgin olive oil.

Sauté the Spanish chorizos for 2 to 3 minutes until the edges are crisp. Remove the chorizos and drain them on paper towels. Set aside.

Sauté the garlic, onions and bell peppers for 2 minutes. Click Cancel to turn off the Sauté button.

Add the chicken, potatoes and carrots to the pot.

Pour in the broth and season with salt and black pepper.

Secure the lid. Check that the cooking pressure is on High and the release valve is set to Sealing.

Select High Pressure* and cook for 40 minutes.

When cooking is complete, use a quick release and carefully open the lid.

Add the heavy cream and the sour cream. Return the chorizos to the pot. Stir slightly to incorporate the cream.

Close the lid. Click Keep Warm for 10 minutes so that all of the ingredients and flavors are blended. Serve in a glass or metal baking dish.

Optional Pie Crust: If desired, roll out a single crust pie pastry (homemade or store-bought). Arrange the chicken pastel in a baking dish. Place the pastry over the dish and seal the edges by pressing down with a fork. Brush the pastry with an egg wash (1 egg beaten with 2 tablespoons water). Bake at a 350° F in a preheated oven for 30 to 35 minutes until the crust is golden brown.

*Note: It takes about 17 to 20 minutes for the Instant Pot® to preheat before the High-Pressure cooking time begins. For other multicookers, please consult the product manual.

INGREDIENTS

2 Tablespoons extra virgin olive oil

2 Spanish chorizos (6 ounces each), sliced

2 garlic cloves, peeled and minced

1 large white or yellow onion, sliced

1 red or green bell pepper, seeded and sliced

4 pounds bone-in chicken (about 6 to 8 pieces), cut up

2 medium potatoes, peeled and quartered

1 medium carrot, peeled and sliced

6 cups organic chicken broth

1 teaspoon salt

1 teaspoon ground black pepper

½ cup heavy cream

½ cup sour cream

Add-On:

1 single crust pie pastry (optional)

SERVINGS: 4
PREP TIME: 20 minutes
PRESSURE: 40 minutes
PRESSURE LEVEL: High. Release
CATEGORY: Moderately Easy

Hardinero

Hardinero

PROCEDURE

In a large mixing bowl, combine the ground pork, ham, green peas, carrots, onions, egg, flour, raisins, soy sauce, tomato paste, salt and ground black pepper. Mix well.

Place the mixture into an oval-shaped llanera or a 7-inch metal round cake pan that fits inside the multicooker. Arrange the slices of hard-boiled egg on top of the meat loaf, pressing down slightly to embed the eggs. Cover the llanera or pan with aluminum foil.

Place the steamer rack inside the pot. Add about 2 cups water, just until it reaches the edges of the rack.

Place the llanera or pan on the steamer rack.

Secure the lid. Check that the cooking pressure is on High and the release valve is set to Sealing.

Select High Pressure* for 35 minutes.

When cooking is complete, use a quick release. Use silicone oven mitts to remove the pan from the pot. Remove the foil wrapping. After the meat has cooled for 5 to 10 minutes, invert the llanera or pan onto a platter to unmold the loaf and to serve.

*Note: It takes about 17 to 20 minutes for the Instant Pot® to preheat before the High-Pressure cooking time begins. For other multicookers, please consult the product manual.

INGREDIENTS

1 pound ground pork

½ cup chopped ham

⅓ cup green peas

½ cup chopped carrots

1 large white or yellow onion, chopped

1 egg

2 Tablespoons all-purpose flour

½ cup raisins

¼ cup soy sauce

2 Tablespoons tomato paste

1 teaspoon salt

1 teaspoon ground black pepper

1 hard-boiled egg, peeled and sliced

SERVINGS: 4
PREP TIME: 15 minutes
PRESSURE: 35 minutes
PRESSURE LEVEL: High. Pressure
CATEGORY: Easy

Kare Kare

Kare Kare

PROCEDURE

To toast the rice flour, select Sauté on high heat. When the inside pot is heated (about 1 minute), add the rice flour. Using a silicone or wooden spoon, stir the flour for 2 to 3 minutes until it turns a light brown color and gives off a toasted aroma. Click Cancel to turn off Sauté. Transfer the toasted rice flour to a small bowl and set aside.

To parboil the oxtails, place the meat, water and half of the garlic and onions in the pot. Season with salt and black pepper. Secure the lid.

Check that the cooking pressure is on High and the release valve is set to Sealing.

Select High Pressure* for 45 minutes. When cooking is complete, use a quick release and carefully open the lid. Using a ladle, remove the oxtails and reserve the broth. Set both aside.

Heat the multicooker again by selecting Sauté on high heat. When the inside pot is heated (about 1 minute), add the vegetable oil. Sauté the remaining garlic and onions for 2 minutes. Click Cancel to turn off the Sauté.

Pour the beef broth and reserved oxtail broth into the pot and add the peanut butter. Blend the peanut butter into the broth until smooth.

Add the toasted rice flour to the broth mixture and stir until there are no more lumps.

(continued on next page)

INGREDIENTS

1 cup rice flour

3 to 4 pounds oxtails, about 6 pieces

6 cups water

4 garlic cloves, peeled and minced—use ½ for parboiling the oxtails, ½ for sautéing

1 ½ large white or yellow onions, chopped and divided—½ for parboiling the oxtails, ½ for sautéing

2 teaspoons salt, divided—1 teaspoon for marinating the oxtails, 1 teaspoon for stewing

2 teaspoons ground black pepper, divided—1 teaspoon for marinating the oxtails, 1 teaspoon for stewing

2 Tablespoons vegetable oil

4 cups beef broth

4 cups oxtail broth (the liquid left from parboiling the oxtails)

1 cup chunky peanut butter

2 Asian eggplants, sliced

2 cups *sitaw* (long green beans), cut into 2-inch pieces

2 cups shredded bok choy

1 cup *bagoong guisado* (sautéed shrimp paste – see Glossary)

SERVINGS: 4
PREP TIME: 1 hour
PRESSURE: 58 minutes
PRESSURE LEVEL: High. Release
CATEGORY: Moderately Easy

Kare Kare

PROCEDURE *(continued from previous page)*

Add the parboiled oxtails, eggplants and sitaw. Season the broth with salt and black pepper.

Secure the lid. Check that the cooking pressure is on High and the release valve is set to Sealing. Select High Pressure* for 7 minutes.

When cooking is complete, use a quick release. Carefully open the lid and stir the ingredients.

Add the shredded bok choy. Secure the lid. Select Keep Warm for 6 minutes. Click Cancel to turn off.

Serve the kare-kare with bagoong guisado on the side.

Note: After the initial Sauté, it takes about 17 to 20 minutes for the Instant Pot® to preheat before the High-Pressure cooking time begins. For other multicookers, please consult the product manual.

Pata Tim

Pata Tim

PROCEDURE

In a large bowl, marinate the pata in soy sauce and calamansi juice. Cover and refrigerate for at least 1 hour.

Coat the bottom of the inside pot of the multicooker with vegetable oil.

Add the pata, garlic, onions, star anise, panocha or brown sugar, bay leaves, black peppercorns and salt. Pour the broth into the pot. Do not stir.

Secure the lid. Check that the cooking pressure is on High and the release valve is set to Sealing.

Select High Pressure* for 45 minutes.

When cooking is complete, use a quick release. Carefully open the lid and stir the ingredients.

Serve warm with steamed rice.

*Note: It takes about 17 to 20 minutes for the Instant Pot® to preheat before the High-Pressure cooking time begins. For other multicookers, please consult the product manual.

INGREDIENTS

4 pounds pata (pork hocks), bone-in and cut into serving pieces

¼ cup soy sauce

1 Tablespoon calamansi or lemon juice

2 Tablespoons vegetable oil

2 garlic cloves, peeled and mashed

1 large white or yellow onion, chopped

3 star anise points (broken from 1 whole piece)

1 (4-ounce) disc panocha or substitute ½ cup dark brown sugar

2 bay leaves

½ teaspoon whole black peppercorns

1 teaspoon salt

6 cups organic beef or chicken broth

SERVINGS: 4
PREP TIME: 10 minutes
PRESSURE: 45 minutes
PRESSURE LEVEL: High. Release
CATEGORY: Easy

Pork Humba

Pork Humba

PROCEDURE

In a medium bowl, soak the black beans in water for 1 hour to soften. When soft, drain the water and set the beans aside.

Add the following ingredients to the inside pot of the multicooker in order, from bottom to top: pork, soy sauce, pineapple juice, broth, garlic, star anise, salt and ground black pepper.

Secure the lid. Check that the cooking pressure is on High and the release valve is set to Sealing.

Select High Pressure* and cook for 30 minutes.

When cooking is complete, use a quick release and carefully open the lid.

Add the brown sugar and the softened black beans. Stir the ingredients.

Close the lid. Press Keep Warm for 7 minutes to blend the flavors.

Garnish with chopped parsley and serve warm with steamed rice.

*Note: It takes about 17 to 20 minutes for the Instant Pot® to preheat before the High-Pressure cooking time begins. For other multicookers, please consult the product manual.

INGREDIENTS

1 cup canned black beans

1 pound pork shoulder or belly, cut into 2-inch cubes

¼ cup soy sauce

¾ cup pineapple juice

2 cups organic beef or chicken broth

4 garlic cloves, peeled and minced

2 to 3 star anise points (broken from 1 whole piece)

½ teaspoon salt

1 teaspoon ground black pepper

¼ cup dark brown sugar

1 Tablespoon fresh parsley, chopped

SERVINGS: 4
PREP TIME: 10 minutes
PRESSURE: 30 minutes
PRESSURE LEVEL: High. Release
CATEGORY: Easy

Pork Siomai

Pork Siomai

PROCEDURE

In a large bowl, combine the pork, scallions, carrots, jicama, egg, flour, soy sauce, rice wine and sesame oil. Season with salt and ground black pepper. Mix the ingredients well.

Arrange the individual wonton wrappers on a dry surface. Place a tablespoon of the pork mixture in the center of each wrapper. Brush the edges of the wrapper with an egg wash (1 egg beaten with 2 tablespoons water). Gather the edges to the center to shape the siomai like an open flower. Repeat until all the wrappers are filled

Place the siomai in a silicone or metal steamer basket that measures 7-inches, or one that fits inside the multicooker pot.

Pour 2 to 3 cups water into the inside pot. Place the trivet or metal rack that comes with the multicooker into the pot. Put the siomai-filled steamer basket on top of the trivet.

Secure the lid. Check that the cooking pressure is on High and the release valve is set to Sealing.

Select High Pressure* and cook for 20 minutes.

When cooking is complete, use a quick release and carefully open the lid.

Use silicone pot holders or mitts to remove the steamer basket.

Serve the siomai with soy sauce and slices of calamansi or lemon.

*Note: It takes about 17 to 20 minutes for the Instant Pot® to preheat before the High-Pressure cooking time begins. For other multicookers, please consult the product manual.

INGREDIENTS

1 pound ground pork

2 scallion stalks, chopped

1 cup chopped carrots

1 cup chopped jicama

1 egg

2 Tablespoons all-purpose flour

2 Tablespoons soy sauce

1 Tablespoon Shaoxing rice wine

⅛ teaspoon sesame oil

1 teaspoon salt

1 teaspoon ground black pepper

20 to 24 wonton wrappers at room temperature

¼ cup soy sauce

2 to 3 calamansi or 1 lemon, sliced

SERVINGS: 4
PREP TIME: 20 minutes
PRESSURE: 20 minutes
PRESSURE LEVEL: High. Release
CATEGORY: Easy

Sinigang na Baboy sa Bayabas at Sampaloc

Sinigang na Baboy sa Bayabas at Sampaloc

PROCEDURE

Preheat the multicooker by selecting Sauté on high heat.

When the inside pot is heated (about 1 minute), add the vegetable oil.

Sauté the garlic and onions for 1 to 2 minutes.

Add the patis and tamarind concentrate.

Click Cancel to turn off Sauté.

Add the pork, guavas, radish and siling mahaba.

Pour the broth into the pot and season with salt and ground black pepper.

Secure the lid. Check that the cooking valve is set to Sealing.

Select High Pressure* and cook for 30 minutes.

When cooking is complete, use a quick release and carefully open the lid.

Add the sitaw and kangkong. Close the lid.

Click Keep Warm for 7 minutes for the sitaw and kangkong to cook in the residual heat.

Click Cancel to turn off.

Serve warm with steamed rice and patis on the side.

*Note: After the initial Sauté, it takes about 17 to 20 minutes for the Instant Pot® to preheat before the High-Pressure cooking time begins. For other multicookers, please consult the product manual.

Cook's comment: If fresh guavas are not available, omit from the recipe.

INGREDIENTS

2 Tablespoons vegetable oil

2 garlic cloves, peeled and minced

1 large white or yellow onion, sliced

2 Tablespoons patis (fish sauce)

½ cup tamarind concentrate

1 pound pork ribs, cut into 2-inch pieces

2 fresh guavas, peeled, seeded and quartered

1 daikon radish, peeled and sliced

2 siling mahaba (mild, finger-like peppers)

8 cups vegetable broth

1 teaspoon salt

1 teaspoon ground black pepper

2 cups sitaw (yardlong beans), cut into 2-inch pieces

2 cups kangkong (water spinach), stems trimmed

¼ cup patis (fish sauce), as a side condiment

SERVINGS: 2 to 4
PREP TIME: 10 minutes
PRESSURE: 30 minutes
PRESSURE LEVEL: High. Release.
CATEGORY: Easy

Desserts and Beverage

Pandan Iced Tea

Pandan Iced Tea

PROCEDURE

Knot the pandan leaves in the middle. Place them on the bottom of the inside pot.

Add the water.

Secure the lid. Check that the cooking pressure is on High and the release valve is set to Sealing.

Select Manual and cook at High Pressure* for 5 minutes.

When cooking is complete, use a quick release and carefully open the lid.

Strain the liquid into a large pitcher.

Stir the calamansi juice and honey into the pandan liquid mixture. Cover and refrigerate. Serve the beverage ice-cold in individual glasses.

*Note: It takes about 17 to 20 minutes for the Instant Pot® to preheat before the High-Pressure cooking time begins. For other multicookers, please consult the product manual.

INGREDIENTS

20 to 25 pieces fresh or frozen pandan (screw pine) leaves

8 to 10 cups water

2 teaspoons calamansi or lemon juice

½ cup honey or brown sugar

SERVINGS: 4
PREP TIME: 7 minutes
PRESSURE: 5 minutes
PRESSURE LEVEL: High. Release
CATEGORY: Quick

Banana-Mango Bread

Banana–Mango Bread

PROCEDURE

Whisk the flour, baking soda and salt in a bowl and set aside.

In another large mixing bowl, cream the butter and sugar with an electric mixer.

Add the eggs one at a time and beat well.

Blend in the mashed bananas and vanilla extract.

Add the flour mixture to the banana mixture and beat the ingredients until the batter is smooth.

Fold the dried mangoes into the batter with a spatula.

Grease a piece of parchment paper and place it on the bottom of a 7-inch round metal or silicone cake pan that will fit inside the multicooker pot. Fill the cake pan up to ¾ full with batter.

Cover the cake pan with aluminum foil and place it on a trivet or rack in the inside pot. Pour 3 to 4 cups water down the side of the inside pot, up to the edge of the trivet.

Secure the lid. Check that the cooking pressure is on High* and the release valve is set to Sealing.

Select Manual. Bake for 50 minutes.

When baking is complete, use a quick release and carefully open the lid.

(continued on next page)

INGREDIENTS

2 cups unbleached all-purpose flour

1 ½ teaspoons baking soda

1 teaspoon salt

½ cup butter (1 stick), softened at room temperature

1 cup brown sugar

2 large eggs

½ cup mashed very ripe bananas

1 teaspoon organic vanilla extract

½ cup chopped dried mangoes

SERVINGS: 4 to 6
PREP TIME: 10 minutes
PRESSURE: 50 minutes
PRESSURE LEVEL: High. Bake
CATEGORY: Easy

Banana–Mango Bread

PROCEDURE *(continued from previous page)*

Pierce the center of the quick bread with the tip of a small knife. If the knife comes out clean, the bread is done.

Using silicone oven mitts or potholders, remove the cake pan from the pot. Cool the quick bread on the counter.

Serve warm or cold.

Note: It takes about 17 to 20 minutes for the Instant Pot® to preheat before the High-Pressure cooking time begins. For other multicookers, please consult the product manual.

Kuchinta

Kuchinta

PROCEDURE

Place the panocha discs in a medium mixing bowl and pour boiling water over them. Mash the discs as they soften and melt thoroughly in the hot water until there are no more solid pieces and the water becomes syrup-like.

Add the annatto powder to the panocha syrup. Blend thoroughly until there are no more lumps. Set aside.

In a large mixing bowl, whisk together the flours and brown sugar. Slowly add the panocha-annatto mixture.

Add the lye water and blend the ingredients well until smooth and free of lumps. Use an immersion blender if needed. Set aside.

Grease small (2-inch diameter) metal or silicone muffin molds with coconut oil. If you don't have small muffin molds, use 2 llaneras (oval pans) or a 7-inch round cake pan that fits the steamer basket in the inside pot.

Using a sieve, pour the mixture into the muffin molds up to ¾ full.

Arrange the muffin molds in a silicone or metal steamer basket that fits the inside pot. Place the basket on top of the trivet that comes with your multicooker.

Pour about 4 cups of water along the sides of the inside pot. The water should reach between the trivet and halfway up the sides of the steamer basket.

Secure the lid. Check that the cooking pressure is on High and the release valve is set to Sealing.

(continued on next page)

INGREDIENTS

2 discs (4 ounces each) *panocha*

2 cups boiling water

1 teaspoon annatto (achuete) powder

1 cup rice flour

⅓ cup all-purpose flour

1 cup dark brown sugar

3 teaspoons lye water

1 cup grated coconut meat

SERVINGS: Makes 16 to 18 pieces
PREP TIME: 10 minutes
PRESSURE: 45 minutes
PRESSURE LEVEL: High. Release
CATEGORY: Easy

Kuchinta

PROCEDURE *(continued from previous page)*

Select Manual and cook at Steam for 45 minutes.

When cooking is complete, use a quick release. Click Cancel to turn off and carefully open the lid.

Pierce the centers of the kuchinta with the tip of a sharp knife. If the knife comes out clean, they are done**. Click Cancel to turn off.

When cooled to room temperature, turn the molds upside down to loosen and release the kuchinta. Refrigerate the kuchinta at least 30 minutes before serving.

Serve chilled or at room temperature with grated coconut sprinkled on top.

Always keep the kuchinta and grated coconut refrigerated until ready to serve.

Note: It takes about 17 to 20 minutes for the Instant Pot® to preheat before the High-Pressure cooking time begins. For other multicookers, please consult the product manual.

**Cook's comments: If the top of the kuchinta is still liquid-like when tested after 45 minutes of cooking time, return the muffin molds, llaneras or pan in the steamer basket to the inside pot. Check that the water level reaches the top of the trivet. Secure the lid again. Check that the cooking pressure is on High and the release valve is set to Sealing. Select Manual and cook at Steam for 10 minutes more.*

Leche Flan

Leche Flan

PROCEDURE

TO MAKE THE CARAMEL: Pour the sugar into a small, heavy stockpot set over medium heat on the stove. It will take about 5 minutes for the sugar to start bubbling, starting at the edges and moving to the center. Tilt the pan around to keep the syrup level. Once the white sugar turns an amber color and is boiling, quickly pour the caramel into the round cake pan or divide equally between the 2 llaneras. Set aside.

In a large mixing bowl, gently whisk the egg yolks. Add the evaporated milk and mix well. Pour in the condensed milk and vanilla extract. Blend the ingredients.

Pour the custard mixture through a sieve placed over the caramel-lined cake pan. If using llaneras, fill each container ¾ full. Cover the flan pan or llaneras with aluminum foil and seal tightly.

Place the steamer rack with handles inside the pot. Fill the inside pot with 2 cups of water, reaching up to the edge of the rack.

FOR EACH LLANERA: Cook one llanera at a time.

FOR A ROUND CAKE PAN: Be sure to use a 7-inch diameter metal pan that fits inside the multicooker. Wrap the bottom of the pan with foil if using a springform pan.

Secure the lid. Check that the cooking pressure is on Manual and the release valve is set to Sealing.

Select Manual and Steam for 20 minutes for each llanera. For a round cake pan, Steam for 25 minutes.

(continued on next page)

INGREDIENTS

1 cup granulated sugar

8 egg yolks

1 (12-ounce) can evaporated milk

1 (14-ounce) can condensed milk

1 teaspoon vanilla extract

EQUIPMENT

Steamer rack with handles (comes with some multicooker models)

7-inch round metal cake pan or 2 llaneras (oval pans about 5 inches long)

SERVINGS: 4 to 6
PREP TIME: 10 minutes
PRESSURE: Manual Steam 20 minutes
CATEGORY: Easy

Leche Flan

PROCEDURE *(continued from previous page)*

When cooking is complete, use a quick release. Carefully remove the flan by using silicone mitts to hold the handles of the steamer rack. Place the flan on the counter to cool. Refrigerate for at least 6 hours or overnight before serving the flan.

*Note: When turning on Steam, it takes about 17 to 20 minutes for the Instant Pot® to preheat before the cooking time begins. For other multicookers, please consult the product manual.

Putong Puti

Putong Puti

PROCEDURE

Grease round metal or silicone *puto* molds (about 1 to 2 inches in diameter) with coconut oil, adding more if needed. Set aside.

In a large bowl, mix the flour, milk, sugar, butter, baking powder and salt. Blend well until the batter is smooth.

Pour batter into each of the molds, filling them ¾ full.

Place the puto molds inside a 7-inch steamer basket that fits inside the multicooker.

Place the trivet that comes with your multicooker in the inside pot and then put the steamer basket on top of the trivet.

Fill the inside pot with 4 cups of water or until the liquid is up to the sides of the steamer basket.

Secure the lid. Check that the cooking pressure is on High and the release valve is set to Sealing.

Select Manual and cook at Steam for 10 minutes.

When cooking is complete, use a quick release and carefully open the lid.

Insert the tip of a small knife into the center of each puto. If the knife comes out clean, the puto is ready.

Remove the steamer basket from the inside pot and cool on the counter for 15 minutes.

(continued on next page)

INGREDIENTS

1 Tablespoon coconut oil

1 cup all-purpose flour

1 cup whole milk

¾ cup granulated sugar

2 Tablespoons melted unsalted butter

2 teaspoons baking powder

½ teaspoon salt

1 cup grated coconut

SERVINGS: 4
PREP TIME: 10 minutes
PRESSURE: 10 minutes
PRESSURE LEVEL: Steam. High
CATEGORY: Easy

Putong Puti

PROCEDURE (continued from previous page)

Gently run a sharp knife around the edges of the steamed puto. Turn over each individual mold to release the puto onto a plate.

Serve warm or chilled and topped with grated coconut meat.

Putong puti and grated coconut must always be refrigerated.

Note: It takes about 17 to 20 minutes for the Instant Pot® to preheat before the High-Pressure cooking time begins. For other multicookers, please consult the product manual.

Cook's comments: Steam the puto in batches if the individual molds do not all fit in the steamer basket at one time. If the puto is still liquid-like and not yet cooked after 10 minutes, return the molds to the steamer basket. Check that the water level reaches the sides of the basket. Secure the lid again. Check that the cooking pressure is on High and the release valve is set to Sealing. Select Manual and cook at Steam for 10 minutes more.

Suman sa Ibus

Suman sa Ibus

PROCEDURE

Soak the malagkit in cold water for 6 hours or overnight in the refrigerator.

Drain the soaked rice and discard the liquid.

Preheat the multicooker by selecting Sauté on high heat.

When the inside pot is heated (about 1 minute), add the malagkit, coconut milk, sugar and salt. Stir to combine the ingredients and continue stirring slowly for about 5 to 6 minutes until the rice becomes puffy and slightly soft.

Turn off the Sauté button by clicking Cancel.

Remove the hot inside pot using silicone pot holders. Transfer the rice mixture to a large bowl. Rinse the inside pot and place it back in the multicooker.

Shape 2 Tablespoons of the rice mixture into thin, 4-inch logs in the center of each banana leaf square. Wrap each suman like a burrito, rolling it away from you and folding both ends inward. Tie each suman with thin strips of banana leaves or butcher's twine. Wrap and tie each piece tightly so that the rice does not burst out while cooking on high pressure.

Place the banana leaf-wrapped suman into a 7-inch metal or silicone steamer basket that fits in the inside pot.

(continued on next page)

INGREDIENTS

1 ½ cups *malagkit* (sweet rice)

1 (14-ounce) can coconut milk

½ cup granulated sugar

¼ teaspoon salt

12 to 14 whole banana leaves, cut into 8-inch squares

SERVINGS: 10 to 12 pieces
PREP TIME: 15 minutes
PRESSURE: 20 minutes
PRESSURE LEVEL: High. Release
CATEGORY: Easy

Suman sa Ibus

PROCEDURE *(continued from previous page)*

Place the steamer basket on top of the rack or trivet that comes with the multicooker. Pour about 2 cups of water into the pot, reaching to the top of the rack.

Secure the lid. Check that the cooking pressure is on High and the release valve is set to Sealing.

Select High Pressure* and cook for 20 minutes.

When cooking is complete, use a quick release. Remove the suman pieces with tongs. Serve warm or chilled, with sugar or fresh ripe mangoes on the side.

*Note: It takes about 17 to 20 minutes for the Instant Pot® to preheat before the High-Pressure cooking time begins. For other multicookers, please consult the product manual.

Ube Haleya

Ube Haleya

PROCEDURE

Grease a 7-inch round metal baking pan or two (5-inch) oval llaneras with coconut oil and butter. Set aside.

If using frozen precooked ube, thaw at room temperature. Do not use a microwave to thaw.

If using fresh ube, place the tubers in the inside pot of the multicooker and add water.

Secure the lid. Check that the cooking pressure is on High and the release valve is set to Sealing.

Select Manual and High Pressure*. Cook for 10 minutes.

When cooking is complete, use a quick release and carefully open the lid.

Use tongs to remove the ube from the pot and transfer them to a large mixing bowl. Discard the liquid in the pot. Set the ube aside to cool for 5 minutes. When cool enough to handle, peel the skin off the softened ube.

Mash the freshly cooked or thawed ube with a potato masher, yielding about 2 cups.

Add the rice flour, sugar, coconut milk, condensed milk and ube flavoring to the mashed ube. Mix with a large wooden spoon until the ingredients are well combined.

Pour the ube mixture into the greased cake pan. If using llaneras, divide the mixture between the two containers and cook each oval pan one at a time.

(continued on next page)

INGREDIENTS

1 ½ pounds fresh ube (about 2 tubers), unpeeled and cut in half, or use 16 ounces frozen precooked ube

3 cups water

1 Tablespoon coconut oil

1 Tablespoon unsalted butter, softened

1 cup rice flour

1 cup granulated sugar

½ cup canned coconut milk

1 (14-ounce) can condensed milk

2 Tablespoons ube flavoring

SERVINGS: 6 to 8
PREP TIME: 10 minutes
PRESSURE: 10 minutes
STEAM: 20 minutes
PRESSURE LEVEL: Steam. High
CATEGORY: Easy

Ube Haleya

PROCEDURE *(continued from previous page)*

Place the pan or llanera on a rack or trivet inside the pot.

Fill the inside pot with 4 cups of water, or until it reaches halfway up the side of the cake pan or llanera.

Secure the lid. Check that the cooking pressure is on High and the release valve is set to Sealing.

Select Manual and Steam for 20 minutes.

If using llaneras, check the amount of water in the pot when cooking each oval pan.

Once cooking is done, use a quick release and carefully open the lid. Using silicone oven mitts, remove the cake pan or llanera. The ube haleya should have a thick, heavy consistency that can coat the back of a spoon.

Place the pan or llanera on the counter to cool. When the ube haleya has cooled to room temperature (about 1 hour), transfer to sterile glass Mason jars. This recipe fills three 12-ounce glass jars.

Always keep ube haleya refrigerated.

Note: It takes about 17 to 20 minutes for the Instant Pot® to preheat before the High-Pressure cooking time begins. For other multicookers, please consult the product manual.

Cook's comments: If fresh ube is not available, frozen precooked ube is sold in Asian markets.

Bibliography

Alejandro, Reynaldo G. *The Philippine Cookbook*. 1985 ed. New York: Coward-McCann, 1982. Print.

Barreto, Glenda Rosales, et al. *Kulinarya: A Guidebook to Philippine Cuisine*. Pasig City, Philippines: Anvil, 2008. Print. Fifth Printing, 2010.

Bernardo, Kristy. *Weeknight Cooking with your Instant Pot®*. Salem, MA: Page Street Publishing Co., 2018. Print.

Besa, Amy, and Romy Dorotan. *Memories of Philippine Kitchens: Stories and Recipes from Far and Near*. New York, NY: Stewart, Tabori & Chang, 2012. Print.

Clark, Melissa. *Dinner in an Instant*. New York, NY: Clarkson Potter Publishers, 2017. Print

David-Pérez, Enriqueta. *Recipes of the Philippines*. Metro Manila: National Book Store, 1973. Print. 19th Printing.

Daza, Nora Villanueva. *Let's Cook with Nora: A Treasury of Filipino, Chinese and European Dishes*. 1975 ed. Manila: National Book Store, 1969. Print.

Editors at America's Test Kitchen. *Multicooker Perfection: Cook It Fast or Cook It Slow – You Decide*. Boston, MA: America's Test Kitchen, 2018. Print.

Fernandez, Doreen, and Edilberto N. Alegre. *Sarap: Essays on Philippine Food*. Aduana, Intramuros, Manila: Mr. & Ms. Pub., 1988. Print.

Gapultos, Marvin. *The Adobo Road Cookbook: A Filipino Food Journey-From Food Blog to Food Truck, and Beyond*. North Clarendon, VT: Tuttle, 2013. Print.

Hester, Kathy. *The Ultimate Vegan Cookbook for Your Instant Pot®*. Salem, MA: Page Street Publishing Co., 2017. Print.

Polistico, Edgie. *Philippine Food, Cooking and Dining Dictionary*. Mandaluyong City, Philippines: Anvil Publishing Inc., 2016. Print.

Randolph, Laurel. *The Instant Pot® Electric Pressure Cooker Cookbook – Easy Recipes for Fast and Healthy Meals*. Berkeley, CA: Rockridge Press, 2016. Print.

Tanumihardja, Patricia. *The Asian Grandmothers Cookbook: Home Cooking from Asian American Kitchens*. Seattle, WA: Sasquatch, 2009. Print.

Glossary

Achuete seeds – also known as annatto, atsuete or achiote; orange-colored seeds used for coloring and imparting a slightly nutty flavor.

Adobo – the unofficial national dish of the Philippines; a tangy stew of meat, seafood or vegetables flavored with vinegar, garlic, bay leaves and peppercorns.

Alimango – crab.

Ampalaya – bitter gourd or bitter melon; also called amargoso in the Philippines.

Asian eggplant – known as talong in the Philippines. Dark purple in color, the slim and long varieties are abundant in the Philippines and most parts of Asia.

Bagoong – fermented fish (isda) or shrimp (alamang) paste; can be sautéed or used as a dipping sauce.

Bagoong guisado – sautéed shrimp paste. For one serving, sauté in 1 tablespoon of vegetable oil: 2 peeled garlic cloves, 1 teaspoon sugar, 1 cup of bagoong alamang and 1 tablespoon of white vinegar.

Banana ketchup – made with pureed banana, salt, sugar, onions, flour and sometimes red food coloring.

Banana leaves – often used in Southeast Asia instead of aluminum foil to wrap food for grilling, steaming or boiling. The large, long leaves render a mild, grassy fragrance and, occasionally, a pale green color to the food. Fresh or frozen leaves are available in Asian markets.

Bangus – milkfish. Plentiful along the coasts and around islands with coral reefs, they have been commercially farmed since the late 1970s and are also found in Indonesia and Taiwan.

Bayabas – guava. A sweet, tropical fruit nearly the size of an apple, it is light green on the outside and has a crisp flesh inside. The seeded inner core can be either light green or red.

Bay leaves – also known as laurel in the Philippines. The aromatic and usually dried leaf of the bay tree is used to enhance flavors when cooking.

Black beans, Chinese salted – soybeans preserved in salt. They develop a dark color, salty flavor and slightly bitter aftertaste through oxidation. Before cooking, soak in hot water for 10 minutes or rinse through several changes of cold water to remove excess salt.

Bok choy – also known as Chinese white cabbage or pak choy; a stir-fry favorite for its pale green, spoon-like stems and dark green leaves. The smaller variety is often referred to as 'baby bok choy' in supermarkets in the USA.

Bola-bola – meatballs.

Calamansi – small Philippine citrus fruit similar in appearance to a kumquat.

Caldero – a large, cast-iron cauldron for stewing food or cooking rice.

Casuy – cashew nuts.

Cider vinegar – made from fermented apple cider.

Chayote – also known as sayote; a pear-shaped vegetable in the same botanical family as squash. It grows in warm climates like Asia, South America and Mexico, and softens when cooked.

Coconut cream – known as kakang gata in the Philippines; the first extracts of coconut cream after hot water is poured over freshly grated coconut meat and then pressed.

Coconut milk – creamy, sweet liquid pressed from freshly grated flesh of mature, brown coconuts. In the USA and countries abroad, good quality canned coconut milk is available in large supermarkets.

Daikon radish – known as labanos in the Philippines; elongated white radish used in Filipino and Japanese dishes.

Dried mango – thin slices of mango preserved with sugar; a popular snack and Philippine export to many parts of the world.

Galapong – glutinous rice ground into flour.

Guinataan – a cooking method using coconut milk or cream.

Guisado – a cooking method akin to sautéing.

Inabraw – from the Ilocano word abraw/abrao; a method of cooking in which fish and vegetables are layered and boiled in shrimp paste.

Kangkong – water spinach; also called swamp cabbage, hollow spinach or morning glory.

Kanin – Tagalog word for rice.

Llanera – a Spanish-derived Pilipino term referring to a deep, oval-shaped metal or tin pan used for making flan. In the USA, they can be found at Asian markets or online sources.

Lye water – known as lihiya in the Philippines; sodium hydroxide, an alkaline substance used in cooking to give a sticky texture and darker color to food.

Malunggay – Moringa oleifera; horseradish leaves used in vegetable dishes.

Manila clams – known as tulya in the Philippines; small, round, white-shelled clams.

Merienda – a snack between meals, usually in the afternoon between lunch and dinner.

Monggo – mung beans; tiny, green, oval-shaped beans used in sweet and savory dishes.

Nilasing na hipon – literally means 'drunken shrimp'; describes a seafood dish in which fresh (sometimes live) shrimp are soaked in wine or beer before cooking in a broth.

Oyster sauce – made from oysters, water and salt; a salty condiment used in many Chinese recipes for meats, seafood and vegetables.

Pancit canton – a Filipino adaptation of Chinese dried noodles, made of wheat flour, coconut oil, and yellow food coloring. The thick, yellow strands are used to make the eponymous dish.

Pandan leaves – also called screwpine. Known as the vanilla of Southeast Asia, the grass-like blades grow up to 2 feet long and have a sweet, floral aroma and slightly herbal taste. Fresh or frozen leaves are sold in Asian markets.

Panocha – a raw sugarcane cake. Reddish-brown in color, it is made from boiled molasses and molded into a round disc resembling a small coconut shell.

Patis – fish sauce; light brown liquid distilled from fermented fish.

Plantains – known as saging saba in the Philippines; a local variety of banana in the Philippines that is usually cooked and has a sweeter taste than fresh ones. Used in both desserts and savory dishes, it can be boiled, steamed or fried. In the USA, fresh or frozen plantains are sold in Asian markets or large supermarkets.

Pork pata – pig's hocks or legs.

Rice flour – ground from regular long-grain rice; used to make rice noodles and savory cakes.

Shaoxing wine – aromatic wine made by fermenting glutinous rice; a standard Chinese cooking spirit used in most stir-fried and braised dishes.

Sili – general term for chili peppers.

Sitaw – yardlong beans.

Soy sauce – made from fermented soybeans and ground wheat. There are many different types manufactured in various Asian countries. Philippine soy sauce (toyo) is used in the recipes of this cookbook.

Spanish chorizo – pork sausages seasoned with paprika, chilies and garlic. Also known as chorizo Bilbao in the Philippines.

Spanish olives – green olives stuffed with pimientos.

Star anise – reddish-brown pods shaped like eight-point stars; imbues braises and stews with an intense licorice flavor and aroma. It is best to remove the pods before serving the dish.

Sweet rice – also known as glutinous rice, sticky rice or malagkit in the Philippines; often used for Filipino kakanin (rice cakes). When cooked, the fat, opaque grains turn translucent and sticky.

Tamarind concentrate – dark, thick liquid or paste from the tamarind fruit. Popular as a souring agent in Southeast Asian cooking, it has a mellow, sweet-tart and tangy flavor.

Tofu – also known as bean curd; a high-protein, low-fat food made from the curds of coagulated fresh soy milk. The curds are pressed together to form cakes that range in texture from soft to extra firm.

Ube – also known as purple yam; a tuber that grows aboveground and is seasonally abundant in Asia during the late months of the year. It resembles a large, long potato on the outside and has lavender flesh inside. Fresh or frozen parboiled ube is sold in Asian markets around the USA and Canada.

Ube flavoring – liquid flavoring of purple yam, with a sweet, almond-like taste and floral aroma; sold in Asian markets or online sources.

Worcestershire sauce - a pungent, dark-colored liquid whose ingredients include soy, vinegar and garlic; added to dishes to increase robust flavors.

About the Author

Elizabeth Ann Besa-Quirino is an author, an award-winning journalist, food writer, and correspondent, and blogs about Filipino and Asian home cooking recipes on her popular website Asian in America (www.AsianInAmericaMag.com). She is a four-time winner of the Plaridel Writing Award for best in journalism, given by the Philippine-American Press Club in San Francisco, CA, and is the recipient of a Doreen Gamboa Fernandez Food Writing Award for her essay, "A Hundred Mangoes in a Bottle." She was named as one of the FWN Filipina Women's Network 100 Most Influential Women of the World in 2013.

Her writing has been published on Positively Filipino, a premier online magazine; FOOD Magazine by ABS-CBN Inc.; Rustan's Sans Rival magalogue; and Philadelphia's Quirk Books Community blog. She has appeared on the TV network KACL-LA 18's "Halo-Halo with Kat Iniba," which aired in California and Hawaii.

Betty Ann, as she is fondly called, was born in the Philippines and raised in Tarlac province, where her way of life was molded early on by her parents' farming and agricultural business. Her childhood home was well known to friends and family as the 'home along the highway', a welcome stopover conveniently halfway between Manila and Baguio. She learned to cook from her mother, Lulu Reyes Besa, who made dishes from the fresh produce grown in their backyard and farm.

Memories of these special meals were the inspiration for her three cookbooks: *Instant Filipino Food: Cooking My Mother's Philippine Recipes in a Multicooker Pot*, *My Mother's Philippine Recipes*, and *How to Cook Philippine Desserts: Cakes and Snacks*.

She has also co-authored the history book *Statesman and Survivor: Elpidio Quirino, 6th President of the Philippines*, and created, illustrated and published *Color and Cook Food Coloring Book* on original Filipino food art. All her books are available on Amazon.com.

Now based in New Jersey, USA, Betty Ann is a member of the International Association of Culinary Professionals and the Association of Culinary Historians of the Philippines. She travels often to the Philippines and throughout Asia in search of traditional recipes and stories about culture and personalities.

OTHER BOOKS BY ELIZABETH ANN BESA-QUIRINO

My Mother's Philippine Recipes (2017)
How to Cook Philippine Desserts (2016)
Color and Cook Food Coloring Book of Filipino Food (2016)
Statesman and Survivor: Elpidio Quirino, 6th President of the Philippines (2015)

Acknowledgments

My deepest gratitude to you, dear readers of my Filipino recipe blog Asian in America. You keep me inspired and motivated to go back to the kitchen and keep cooking. I enjoy hearing from all of you and when you share with me what you have cooked from my cookbooks, my blog or feature articles, I am touched and honored.

I always tell folks that publishing a cookbook is similar to giving birth. There are highs and lows and the last weeks are nerve-wracking and nail-biting times. But I wouldn't have been able to survive the last few months without the wonderful people in my life who are there for me unconditionally.

To my loving husband, Elpi, our sons, Tim and Constante, thank you for putting up with my anxieties, rants, frustrations, endless questions while simultaneously sharing in the joys and happiness when the sun is shining in my corner.

To my sister, Isabel, my cousins, aunts, uncles, nieces, nephews of the Besa and Quirino clans and all my extended families who believe in me and continue to cheer me on when I need it most.

To my dearest best friends Veng, Tepton, Lily, Irene who were my former classmates in college, my supportive St. Paul's University (SPCM) classmates and alumni, my teachers and professors from my schooldays, my neighbors, and even strangers who come and talk to me about my cookbooks or blog, I will always be grateful for your kind support.

To my outstanding editorial and design team: copy editor Paola Paska, designer Charissa Wilson of Triple Latte Design, and photographer and assistant editor Constante G. Quirino, where would this cookbook be without you? Thank you for your loyalty, your exceptional expertise, all the love and friendship.

To my ever-patient team of recipe testers from New York, New Jersey, Philadelphia, California and all the way to Canada who opened their homes and kitchens to my recipes and ideas led by my wonderful sister-in-law Alicia Quirino-Jacinto, who eagerly savored every recipe I sent and shared the Instant Pot®-love.

To my colleagues, mentors and heroes in the writing and culinary world who I admire: Mona Lisa Yuchengco, Gemma Nemenzo and the Positively Filipino family, Monica Bhide, Dianne Jacob, Nancie McDermott, Jenni Field, Denise Vivaldo, Kathy Hester, Liren Baker, Namiko Chen, Domenica Marchetti, Marcos Calo Medina, Nana Ozaeta, Ige Ramos, Claude and Mary Ann Tayag, Poch Jorolan and the Jorolan family, Joey de Larrazabal-Blanco, Marvin Gapultos, Kho Kian Lam, Pat Tanumihardja, Kristy Bernardo, Johanna Mirpuri, Joanne Boston-Kwanhull and the Filipino Food Movement.

And most of all, to you, dear reader, as you hold this cookbook with your hand and your heart, please know I am grateful to you for having faith in me.

Thank you for joining me in the kitchen and sharing the love of my recipes with your families and friends.

Maraming salamat po! Kain na!

Made in the USA
Middletown, DE
17 December 2019